The Olive Principle

Finding Your Way Back to God

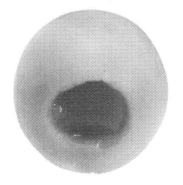

Daniel R. Dorey

iUniverse, Inc.
Bloomington

The Olive Principle
Finding Your Way Back to God

It should be noted that scriptures quoted in this book are taken from the New American Standard Bible, unless otherwise notated.

iUniverse books may be ordered through booksellers or by contacting:

iUniverse
1663 Liberty Drive
Bloomington, IN 47403
www.iuniverse.com
1-800-Authors (1-800-288-4677)

ISBN: 978-1-4502-7774-7 (sc)
ISBN: 978-1-4502-7775-4 (dj)
ISBN: 978-1-4502-7776-1 (ebk)

Library of Congress Control Number: 2010918356

Printed in the United States of America

iUniverse rev. date: 12/29/2010

To my wife, Shelly, who holds me before the Lord daily; my Cornerstone family, who continued to pray for me and encouraged me during the writing of this book; and to Andy and Tiffany Stump, who worked tirelessly in the editing process.

I am like a green olive tree in the house of God;
I trust in the mercy of God forever and ever.
I will praise You forever, Because You have done it;
And in the presence of Your saints
I will wait on Your name, for it is good.
—Psalm 52:8–9 (New King James Version)

Contents

Preface

The idea for this book first came from a conversation that I had with my pastor, Bill Lay, at Cornerstone Church in Grove, Oklahoma. Pastor Lay and I were brainstorming on how to recruit people to be mentors and coaches for new converts to Christianity. Pastor Lay said something to the effect of, "Dan, if you can figure out how to overcome the 'I' problem of people—putting themselves first before they put themselves out, then you will have solved one of the greatest problems plaguing the Body of Christ." As a retired police officer who'd spent his career solving people-generated problems, the task seemed to be a worthy, intriguing challenge. I began to take the matter to the Lord in prayer. The Holy Spirit spoke into my heart that there was a cure for self-first or the "I factor." The Holy Spirit explained to me the need for guidance for established Christians who had fallen away and now longed for Jesus to become their first love again. I was shown "the olive principle," and how the purpose of an olive holds a key to God's purpose for our lives.

In addition, I am repeatedly approached by other believers in search of books that will help them draw closer to God, perhaps because they know that I have a passion for both reading and learning. The passion to study God's Word and to continuously read other books was instilled in me by my former professor and mentor, Dr. Larry Hunt. Dr. Hunt made it clear that if you are not reading several books a month, then you will stagnate, and a stagnated teacher has nothing fresh to say.

Many books, unfortunately, are written in the format of an intellectual theological exercise and are therefore dry as bones to many people. In my search, I have read many books by men I consider to be great biblical scholars, such as Ignatius, Alfred Edersheim, Smith Wigglesworth, Charles Spurgeon, A. W. Tozer, Dietrich Bonhoeffer, and Michael J. Wilkins. I have also read a few books by authors I deemed to be out in left field, or whose writing was so shallow that it offered no real value. My quest has been to find helpful authors that are somewhere in the middle-of-the-road—authors that offer both sound biblical theology and practical application for people's particular needs. Believers must remember that the purpose of extra reading is to complement our primary study of the Bible in search of God's truth. I believe our all-knowing God not only gave us His inspired and infallible Word to guide our lives, but He also gifted men and women within the Body of Christ to search out the deeper mysteries. For those looking for guidance but who don't have four hours a day to devote to study, insightful, practical scholars can present nuggets of truth for practical application.

For these reasons, and because of my desire to serve the Body of Christ, I wrote *The Olive Principle*—not because I have all the answers, but because I have been where so many others are now struggling. I know how it feels to be so deeply in love with the Lord that you can think of nothing else. I have also experienced the unseen force that gradually draws you away from His presence. I know how the pursuit of personal fulfillment and the craziness of daily life can handcuff you and not allow you to see the light at the end of the tunnel. Finally, I too have looked up from under the overwhelming pressures of life and not felt the presence of God.

The Olive Principle is designed to be a complement to your study of Scripture. It is written through the eyes of a person just like you and not through the eyes of an intellectual who is unable to communicate practical solutions. If I've been successful, you will hear yourself saying, "I get it!" I believe that all Christian books should have the same goal as the Bible, and that is to help you along the path to spiritual maturity. Remember that when you join a Christian author on a journey, you have to open your heart to the message and then always check it against the Word of God.

The Olive Principle takes you back through your mind's eye to when you first fell in love with Jesus as your personal Savior. Do you remember the smile that was always on your face? Do you remember how all you could think about was your Master Jesus, and how His glory shined on you? The memory of that close encounter with Jesus is locked deep within your mind and is an experience that no one can ever steal from you. The Bible gives us examples of others who have had such close encounters with the Lord and how the experiences changed their lives just as it changed yours.

For some of you, however, your closeness began to fade, as though some unknown force began to draw you away from the presence and sense of fulfillment once felt in the Lord. Different things or events might have been responsible for shifting your focus and the resulting I factor of putting yourself first before putting yourself out. Is there an outside force luring us, a force that uses the same tactics as a thief?

The Olive Principle will lead you to look through the eyes of an experienced investigator and the method he uses to uncover the truth behind the deception. You will be led just as in a mystery novel to a place where you will come face-to-face with the absolute truth: there is no escape from it. Facing the truth is only the beginning of the journey for those who hunger for fulfillment in God.

Next, you must understand the hidden principle of the olive and how God uses daily circumstances to bring every believer to a place of maturity. There is much to be learned from the process an olive tree must go through in order to bear fruit. The olive can only fulfill its divine purpose when it willingly leaves the safety of the branch and trusts itself to the farmer's hand.

With the olive principle fresh in memory, you are taken along with two imperfect people who underwent the same process as the olive tree. Examples illustrate the process that must be undergone to prepare us for God's purpose in our lives.

Understanding the process leads to a worn and proven trail for those who dare to travel back into the presence of God. The trail is that traveled by Israel when coming out of bondage; it requires the traveler to make tough decisions along the way and to die to self. Making the journey along the proven trail safely guides you to a place of personal commitment and the steps needed to build the discipline required as a servant of God.

Finally, it is only when you understand the true meaning of being a servant that fulfillment is realized in God. There is an attitude that must be grasped in order for you remain in His presence. This place is where you literally become a reflection of Him. Are you ready?

Chapter One:
Do You Remember?

Do you remember what it felt like when you first came to know Jesus as your personal Savior? Do you remember how your face shined with a type of glory, and how you could not get that middle-school grin off your face? Do you remember how you could not get enough of the Bible, and how you told everyone you knew about Jesus, regardless of whether he wanted to hear? Take just a moment and close your eyes and allow your mind's eye to take you back to that time. I would guess that right now you have that silly grin back on your face and that tingle in your heart like the first time you fell in love. Do you remember?

I remember one evening when I arrived at work at the Northeast Oklahoma Police Department, where I had been employed for nineteen years. I was confronted by the records clerk with the question, "Hey Lieutenant, what's going on? There is something different about you." The question caught me off guard. Firstly, because I was known as a focused person who was always on a mission, and secondly, because I strived to show no emotion around those with whom I worked (Mr. Spock on *Star Trek* was my hero).

> **I knew the voice was that of Jesus, whom I had come to know just the evening before.**

The records clerk, Mona, said, "Dan, your face is shining, and you don't have the scowl on your forehead that we're used to seeing." (Mona was a Christian lady who made a habit of avoiding me, as I had a history of coming into her office, grunting orders, and walking out.) I went to look in a mirror to see the difference in my demeanor that seemed so obvious to others. I saw something that put me back on my heels, along with a smile and true look of peace on my face. It was at this time I heard a small voice inside of me say, "It is because I am now part of your life." I knew the voice was that of Jesus, whom I had come to know just the evening before.

I remember being forced to take the life of another human being one evening in September of 2000, as several officers and I were attempting to stop a possible drunk driver in a pickup. Upon stopping the pickup, the male driver exited and charged my squad car, brandishing a knife while cursing at me. This man made two lunges toward me as I commanded him to drop the knife and attempted to get my squad car between us. The man, I thought with the second lunge, had accomplished his goal of stabbing me in the chest. At this point in time I was forced to shoot and kill the man, to not only protect myself, but also the other officers running up to the scene. I felt numb and empty inside.

Even though I was cleared of this event as a justified shooting and went right back to work (back on the horse, so to speak), I continued to feel an emptiness inside. During my career, I had been involved in drug investigations and had taken part in many drug raids, and I was proud of the fact that I'd never had to shoot or kill anyone. Every day after the shooting, I put on my leather "lieutenant face" and went to work, while slipping further and further into a deep depression. After several months of sleeping only an hour or two a night and never leaving the house except for work-related activities, I felt desperate. I cried out to this "God" I had been told about at different times in my life. Something inside was telling me to talk to a pastor, a man I knew from a time in my past when I'd been seeking something more. I never took to the Bible or the church thing, being both self-centered and self-reliant; my pride prevented me from having my emptiness filled.

One day I decided it was worth the risk of letting my guard down just once in order to get some advice from this pastor. I hoped to make peace with whatever was eating me alive like a cancer. I drove the few blocks to this pastor's home, sat on his couch, and told my story. I was disappointed, to say the least, when he did not have any magical formula for me to feel good about myself. Instead, he handed me a key to his church. The pastor said, "Dan, you need to go talk to the only one who can help you—Jesus Christ." I was given instructions on how to go up to the altar, get down on my knees, and ask Jesus for help. Arriving at the church, I went up to the altar and did as I was told. Three hours later, I was on my face bawling and asking for forgiveness for my past. I remember the amazing thing was that when I got up I felt a peace inside of me that I had never felt before, and there was something different about my heart—it felt clean.

So here I was at work and people were telling me I looked different. I went into Mona's office and shut the door (probably to her dismay) and told her that I had surrendered my life to Jesus Christ the night before. I then asked her what to do next. After Mona finished hugging and squeezing the air out of me, she told me to go buy a Bible to begin reading, and that I needed to start going to church.

I went to the local Christian bookstore and bought a Bible (the New International Version), and began reading it from cover to cover. I became one of those maniac Christians: Do you remember what it was like? Do you remember being terribly excited and making sure that everyone heard about your Jesus? I spent every free minute reading my Bible and other books on prayer, fasting, and how to live a holy life. I just could not get enough of God and could do nothing but smile and tell Him over and over again how much I loved Him. The change was earthshaking for an old seasoned cop, especially one who'd become pretty cold and indifferent to people's pain, and who worked hard to show no emotion while on duty (or in his private life). I repeatedly read Psalm 63:1–6,

> O God, you are my God, earnestly I seek you;
> my soul thirsts for you, my body longs for you,
> in a dry and weary land where there is no water.

I have seen you in the sanctuary and beheld your power and your glory. Because your love is better than life, my lips will glorify you. Thus will I bless thee while I live: I will lift up my hands in thy name. My soul shall be satisfied as with marrow and fatness; and my mouth shall praise thee with joyful lips; when I remember thee upon my bed, and meditate on thee in the night watches. (NIV)

I got it! I understood how the writer of this psalm felt. I once again could not sleep, as I was in love with God and had difficulty thinking about anyone or anything else, and my face shined. Do you remember?

In my hunger to identify with the Bible I did a character study of Moses in Exodus 34:29–35. I thought hard about how he would go up on Mount Sinai and stay in the presence of God and when he descended, his face would shine so that it frightened the other Israelites, and he was forced to wear a veil. Moses knew what it felt like to have a real and personal relationship with the Creator of the heavens and earth. Moses could not hide the outward manifestation of God's inward presence from shining on his face. Moses, however, did not always have the glory of God shining on his face. He actually was a murderer and fugitive hiding out from the law (the Egyptians) while herding stupid, smelly sheep in the hot dry desert for his father-in-law. One day while Moses was herding those smelly sheep, he wondered about the purpose of his life and if this was the best he could expect. As he did so, he came across a burning shrub near Mount Horeb, known also as the Mountain of God. It was not unusual to see a shrub or grass burning in this land of burning sand, but this time, the burning bush was not being consumed. As an old cop, I can imagine that Moses just had to see for himself what this was all about, and here he met the Lord. God spoke to Moses audibly in a voice of such authority that it literally shook Moses's world in way from which he would never recover. I believe the Lord could have spoken to Moses with a small voice (as He has with so many of us), and it would not have mattered.

Another biblical example of someone having a life-changing encounter with God can be found in the book of Isaiah 6:1–7. In this passage, Isaiah, who many scholars agree was only a teenager, literally saw the fabric of heaven pulled back so that he might see the very throne of God. Can you imagine the look on Isaiah's face, or how your face would appear at such an event? In verse 1b we read, "I saw the Lord sitting on a throne, lofty and exalted, with the train of His robe filling the temple." Then in verses 2 and 3 we read of Seraphim flying back and forth, crying out like thunder, "Holy, Holy, Holy, is the Lord of hosts, The whole earth is full of His glory." I only imagine Isaiah saw millions of angels around the throne with the glory of God literally brighter than any sun in his face. Isaiah cried out that he was ruined! Just imagine what it would be like to see the curtains of heaven pulled back so God could speak to you personally. Think of how overwhelmed you would feel before Him, and how you would reflect His glory on your face.

The only and (very inadequate) reference point I would have in my personal experience occurred when I lived in Italy and

President Nixon came to the NATO base where my father was a command sergeant major. I was about thirteen years old and stood there with my mouth hanging open in awe, as this was the president of the United States! I remember how I could not wait to tell my other American friends, and some of the Italian kids with whom I played soccer, about the privilege of seeing the most powerful man in the world. In reflection, I realized that he, too, was created and not the Creator.

> **Right there in front of hundreds of people, the Holy Spirit decided to speak into my life.**

I also remember a period of time when I was a children's pastor (talk about herding little sheep), and I was always searching for object lessons to bring the gospel of Jesus alive to my young charges. Once, while attending Church of the Harvest Children's Camp in Oklahoma City and taking the kids to the Omni-Dome Science Exhibit, I discovered a device that reacted to solar power. I had a "eureka" moment as I tried this little device out in the gift store; as you brought it closer to a light source, its inner mechanism would begin to spin. I was like a little kid watching as the device spun faster and faster, the closer it got to the source. Right there, in front of hundreds of people, the Holy Spirit decided to speak into my life. The Holy Spirit reminded me of Moses's face, shining when he got near God, and how my face shined when I stayed near God. This device was an example of the same principle: the closer it is to the source (God), the more power that is generated within. The Holy Spirit reminded me again of the shine on my face, which was the outward manifestation of the presence of God living inside me, His very own creation. I am further reminded of what the German theologian Dietrich Bonhoeffer wrote in his book *The Cost of Discipleship*: "God created Adam in his own image, as a climax of his creation. He wanted to have the joy of beholding in Adam the reflection of himself." It is God's plan for us, who were made just below Him, to reflect the brilliance of who He is. The apostle Paul also tells us in 2 Corinthians 3:18, "But we all, with unveiled face beholding as in a mirror the glory of the Lord, are being transformed into the same image from glory to glory, just as from the Lord, the Spirit." Do you get it? We were created to reflect, just as a mirror, the glory of God on our faces—this is His desire.

The fanatical, overwhelmed part of me had to go tell everyone about this person Jesus that I'd met. At the police department I supervised the evening shift, and the officers and dispatchers did not, in their opinion, really have a choice about hearing the gospel. I was determined (even though I only knew enough to be dangerous) that I was going to snatch people out of the hand of the devil. In reflection, it made me kind of suspicious that during this time in my early Christian life, these folks were always really busy or had to leave and check on a situation. I would never have believed that their other obligations arose because I approached them and shared something I had learned reading the Bible. I had forgotten how we would make fun of people after they tried to witness to us at the police department. (You must understand, we thought we were tough, macho cops who depended only on our own strength.)

While doing another biblical character study, I made a connection with a real-life fanatic, one who'd been kind of a religious cop, and who had persecuted the bothersome Christians. Saul, as he was known, came to meet Jesus through a close encounter on the road to Damascus and got knocked off his high horse (so to speak), which was exactly what happened to me. In Acts 9:20, the Bible tells us how shortly after Saul's encounter with Jesus, "immediately he began to proclaim Jesus in the synagogues, saying, 'He is the Son of God.'" Throughout this chapter we see that Saul was upsetting the worldly Jews so much that they tried to kill him in Damascus. Again in verse 29, we see that Saul went up to Jerusalem to hang out with the apostles, and the Jews tried to kill him. Their belief was that their only choice was to get Saul out of the way until he could be "seasoned" and learn how to correctly approach non-Christians. It is disturbing how many times I have heard church folk say that new Christians need to be locked in a closet for a time until they settle down, "like the rest of us." I believe that this type of thought is just shameful, to be blunt. Rather, we should follow the example found in Acts 18. A newcomer, Apollos, was challenging the unbelieving Jews, when Priscilla and Aquila took him under their wing and mentored him. The plan of Priscilla and Aquila was not to stop Apollos, but to tap into the energy of his belief and teach him about Jesus so that he would be ready to correctly present the gospel. We should all want to follow this example in mentoring and teaching new believers how to both stay in the presence of God so their face continues to reflect His glory and how to properly present the gospel.

Do you remember what it was like to have that feeling of power inside, to have that shine on your face, and to be a fanatic for Jesus? Well, if you are like me and are reading this book, the depth of your feeling diminished—something gradually happened and you drew away from the source. I believe that "something" is what I am going to discuss next and will refer to as the "I factor."

Chapter Two:
The "I Factor"

What possibly could have happened to cause you to look up and not feel the power of God's presence as you once did in your life? Whatever this was, it undoubtedly acted gradually, and either deceived you or found a method to draw you away from the presence of God. You would never willingly turn your back on Him. Let us take a few moments and look at some possible scenarios. Ask yourself whether any of these sound familiar to what has happened in your life.

Scenario #1: You have been working hard your entire adult life and want to see some fruit from all the effort. Your neighbor just bought a brand-new boat and your wife or husband wants to know why your family does not have a boat to go out and enjoy on the lake. Maybe something just keeps nagging at you, "Why don't you buy a new boat? You work hard, you deserve it, and it will give you prestige."

Scenario #2: Your kids are constantly coming home from school and telling you how it is not fair that Brittany in their class gets to have a cell phone, or Puma sneakers, or is always wearing something from a name-brand outfitter. You want your kids to fit in. When you were growing up, you had to do without or wore hand-me-downs from an older sibling. As a good parent, you want your kids to have more than you did growing up.

Scenario #3: You have been in ministry for years: are a former minister, a gifted teacher, or a vocalist whom the Lord has led to another church. There is excitement at first, as everyone is telling you how much the organization can use your gifts and experience; however, after only a few months your gifts have not been employed with the organization's ministry. Basically, you feel that you've been put on a shelf to sit and gather dust.

Scenario #4: You have been sitting in a pew for years and out of the blue someone tries to talk you into serving in ministry. You try to build excuses, as you've never been trained to do anything like this—what do they expect of you anyway?

Scenario #5: You have started and built a ministry within your church. It takes up a great deal of your free time each week to prepare and make contact with those to whom you minister. Now the leadership is asking you to take your valuable time and help with another area of need.

Scenario #6: You work hard all week long and then have to spend Saturday mowing the lawn or attending to the honey-do list hanging on the refrigerator. Something just keeps whispering in your ear, "Why is it wrong for you to miss Sunday morning worship to go motorcycle riding, fishing, or boating, after you worked all week and had to spend Saturday doing chores? Do you think God did not rest from His work?"

Scenario #7: Watching television, you turn to a channel that has a seductive sex scene on it and reason that the pastor hasn't said anything against this particular channel, so it must be okay just this once. The problem is that once turned into frequent viewings of sex-related movies and now you are addicted to pornography.

Scenario #8: You gave your life to Jesus many years ago or have attended church now for years, but have stopped growing in your faith. The service is predictable: you sing two hymns, sit down, take up the offering while you sing a third hymn, followed by an uninspired sermon much like the one the week before. You're thinking about why you waste your time getting up each Sunday morning and going to church.

Is there a plan to get you offtrack and one day discover that the power of God is gone from your life? The method of our drifting away is like that of a burglar "casing a job." The thief watches a house on several different occasions and at different times of day or night. He looks for the habits of the owners and also for a weak place to make entry. Once the thief decides there is the possibility of success (most likely when you are not home), he first quietly approaches, pauses, draws closer, pauses, and so on. The thief will stop and listen for any evidence of your presence. After the thief has found a weak place to make entry into the home, he gradually pries open a door or window, pausing, listening, pausing, and all to avoid being discovered. Once the thief is inside, he is able to gather up and make off with your treasure, and when you come home everything is gone! You ask yourself a thousand questions: did I not lock the door, or set the alarm system, or not pay attention to someone watching?

The problem for most of us is that as something gradual begins to happen, it is subtle, and often goes unnoticed, until one day we look up and do not see God. The fifteenth-century cleric Thomas à Kempis addressed Satan's subtle philosophy in his book, *The Imitation of Christ*. He wrote, "At first it is a mere thought confronting the mind; then imagination paints it in stronger colours; only after that do we take pleasure in it, and the will makes a false move, and we give our assent. It is all so gradual, this wholesale infiltration of our malignant enemy; and because of this we put up no resistance at the start."

In Genesis chapter 3 we read, "the serpent was more crafty than any beast of the field." What did Satan do? I guarantee you he watched Adam and Eve every day at different times to figure out how and when to approach these two unsuspecting lovers of God. You see, Adam and Eve were in love with their Creator, and He was reflected in their faces. So why, when they felt so secure and in love with Him, would they ever need to be alert for an enemy? It was thus easy for Satan to present his philosophy of deception, taking God's Word out of context and leading his targets into error, sin, and death. Satan tells Eve in verse 1, "Indeed, has God said, 'You shall not eat from any tree of the garden.'" Satan challenges what Eve knows to be true, but then appeals to her personal desire, telling her God does not want her to eat of the fruit because she will be just like Him. This is a subtle way of saying, "God does not want you to feel fulfilled and have significance in your life; if He really loved you, He would want you to have all that He possesses." It is here in Genesis that Satan unveils his three-point attack for the fall of man: the lust of the flesh, the lust of the eyes, and the boastful pride of life. Satan is always there to plant the seed of deception, and with time we mistakenly accept sin as the norm for our way of life.

Jesus gives us an example of the result of this type of deception as it affected the rich young ruler found in Matthew 19:16–26. We read that this fine young man was doing all the right things, and he even spoke what I call "Christianese." The young ruler was not murdering his neighbor or stealing, he went to church, paid his tithes and offerings, and probably showed up for fellowship night at his local synagogue. The man ran into a snag, however, when Jesus asked him to follow Him, which meant he had to lay down all his personal "I" plans and get rid of his toys and submit to Jesus's direction for his life. Do you think this young man just began this way? I believe this was a gradual and probably unnoticed change in him. The young man had begun to place his faith in his wealth and not in God. The result was that the young man's wealth was now his god instead of the Lord and he could only serve one master.

Jesus gave another example how of this deception works in a parable well known to anyone who has read the Gospel of Matthew. This is the parable of the sower of seed. I am going to look only at the third point Jesus taught as recorded in Matthew

13:7, which says, "And others fell among thorns, and the thorns came up and choked them out." In laymen's terms this means that we are planted in good soil and in love with God, but the cares of the world enter and choke out our closeness. Weeds do not choke out other plants overnight, but slowly grow, gaining strength until one day they dominate and drain the strength out of the surrounding plants.

The examples help us understand how easy it is to get caught up in finding fulfillment in possession or to get worn down by the cares of life. As I mentioned, the process does not happen overnight and can even take months or years. With this in mind, let's take another look at the scenarios mentioned earlier.

You work hard, take care of your family and just want to have some nice things to enjoy like your neighbor. The desire to have nice things is not wrong and is not generated by a wrong attitude. But did you find yourself wanting more and more over time and finding ways to justify these desires to yourself? The possessions make you feel like you have significance and for the first time in a long time, people are noticing you.

The same can be said about wanting a better life for your kids than you had growing up. As children, both my wife and I did without the nicer clothing and possessions of other children. It is a constant struggle, emotionally and spiritually, when your kids want to wear name-brand clothing or want a new cell phone like the other kids. You do not want your kids to stand out like you did, and you work hard to provide a good life for them. Therefore, it is troubling when other parents spend, spend, spend on their children's every whim, and you try to maintain moderation or have to say no. Have you been worn down and started giving in to your kids? Everyone else does.

Some of you are in a full-time position serving God and your fellow believers, which made your life full and rewarding. Then God moves you and you find yourself sitting on the sidelines like a backup quarterback. You fight the feelings of disappointment that begin to surface, and if you are not careful you begin to dwell in your own disappointment. With time you find yourself losing interest and drawing away from God and church.

How hard would it be for you to sit in a pew for months or years and feel like you are invisible? You never are asked personally to help with any project and thoughts of just staying home begin to surface. Now, someone walks up out of the blue and wants you to serve in a ministry. Do you feel unprepared, untrained, unwilling, and just want to hide somewhere? Do you just want to say no because no one has bothered to include you before?

Are you one of those busy people who pour yourself into a particular ministry? You spend hours and hours sacrificing time away from your family to make your ministry a success. The ministry is growing, you need help, and are at times feeling drained physically, emotionally, and spiritually. Then one day someone in leadership asks you to both lead your ministry and help in another, because no one will step up to the plate. Are you not supposed to feel frustrated or to think about walking away from ministry for a while? You begin to spend less time preparing and start to pull away from other responsibilities, and then you start talking about stepping away from ministry altogether. Why can't you have some time for yourself?

In another scenario, you work hard at your job all week long and have been serving God faithfully in both attendance and in a ministry. On the weekends there is that honey-do list on the refrigerator that just will not go away. You feel worn out from work and chores, as there never seems to be any time to relax. Every time you think about taking some personal time just to rest or take your family on a weekend mini-vacation, you feel guilty about missing church. Is it really wrong to take a weekend off every so often? You take that one weekend, which turned into two and three, and now you've found yourself attending church only once in awhile.

Perhaps you were always determined to do what was right in the eyes of God. There was never any gray area in your sense of right and wrong. But now you have kids, and they are being affected by peer pressure to look and act like the other kids. Your daughter wants to wear clothes to look like the other girls and does not understand that these clothes are seductive and will compromise her integrity. What do you do? Perhaps your son is playing at another believer's home, and he finds the Harry Potter witchcraft movies harmless. Do you compromise your personal integrity to make everyone happy? This problem has worn you down and caused you to give in just this once, which turned into another and another compromise. With time, letting your principles slide has gotten easier.

You watch television when you have time, and on occasion you have the house all to yourself, so giving the remote a workout you look for something interesting. You always have to be on guard with your kids to ensure they are not watching distasteful shows. Just this once you catch yourself watching a hot sex scene on a regular network channel and now that image is in your mind every day. Something inside just keeps urging you to take another peek, and this time the images are more seductive and a feeling of lust is growing inside. You have to keep this to yourself, as people at church would not understand that this makes you feel alive.

Finally, you have been fighting feelings of boredom and discontentment with church. You sing the same old outdated hymns in the same traditional order, which does not draw you into the throne room to worship. Next your pastor gets up and preaches the same uninspired sermons, with nothing to make you search out the deeper things of God. Basically, you have for months (or even years) walked out of church uninspired each Sunday and are sick of the traditionalism. Your church does not offer any classes to teach you how to dig out the nuggets within God's Word, but only the same old devotional-style Sunday school classes taught for new believers. Thoughts regularly surface to the effect that since you are not getting fed anyway, why read your Bible or pray? You begin making the joke that you just want to make it to heaven and are losing interest in moving forward. This loss of interest has caused you to attend church less regularly, and although you say you still know God, you are no longer in love with Him.

All of these types of thoughts come upon you gradually and one way or the other, they find a way to make you think of your (or your family's) desires first. I know that you did not plan to allow something to pull at you and bring confusion into your life. But, is there another one to blame for all these feelings and problems? Is there someone who whispers approval of these ideas in your ear?

> **A corrupt society and a silent**
> **Body of Christ give birth**
> **to spiritual cripples.**

The reality is that this is a plan of deception by Satan to do unto you the same thing he did to Adam and Eve. Today you and your kids sit in front of the television and are brainwashed into believing that you must be wealthy, beautiful, and popular, in order to have real fulfillment in your lives. We wonder why so many adults and children in our society today think only of themselves. The brainwashing of society, and a silent Body of Christ, has given birth to spiritual cripples. These unfortunate people go through life not realizing what is wrong with them. But, you have to ask yourself, is it really their fault?

The Holy Spirit revealed to me all the scenarios discussed earlier, and they are perfect examples of the insidiousness of the I factor. The I factor is putting oneself first, before God and others, as we would rather put ourselves first before putting ourselves out. Through the gradual process of deception, we are led into thinking we should put "self" on the throne and keep God around to serve up some eternal life.

In this chapter I have tried to follow the guidance of the Holy Spirit and reveal the evidence of Satan's evil plan to change each of us into self-first creatures. Satan wants to steal your relationship with God from you. Can you identify with Satan's tempting you with the need for toys or money to feel significance in your life? Is it your fault? Where do you stand? In the next chapter I will discuss the different areas with which you might identify, and how to overcome all of Satan's tricks of the trade.

Chapter Three:
Where Do You Stand?

In the previous chapter I discussed the I factor, and in this process explained the different ways that the old serpent has drawn people to develop the attitude of self-first (humanism). (Humanism, in this book, will refer to a way of life centered on human, rather than spiritual, interests and values.) Remember, he used the lust of the flesh, the lust of the eyes, and a boastful pride of life in order to deceive and to draw mankind—especially Christians—away from God's purpose. My purpose was to show you where you stand in your relationship with God.

While I was in investigations with the police department, we spent a lot of time interrogating suspects for different crimes. There are techniques that have been developed to assist in obtaining confessions or admissions from people who are suspected of committing a crime. One of the techniques used is to present the suspect with different options of how a crime may have been committed and his particular level of involvement. The point of this technique is to allow the individual to "save face," but still admit his guilt. The technique ask questions like: You really did not plan on stealing those fishing poles out of that boat, did you? It was kind of a lapse in judgment, right? Another question might be: You were just riding around in Johnny's car and did not think he was going to actually rob that convenience store, did you? As an interrogator, I would get the suspect to "buy into" one of these varying scenarios as to why he was there and how he was involved, using his self-interest against him. Finally, I would ask the suspect to tell me what really happened.

I showed you how the gradual process of losing one's devotion to God is like that of a burglar's casing a job to make sure that it is possible to break into the victim's home and steal his stuff. The process involves making subtle moves in order to avoid getting caught. Once the burglar has made entry, he is going to steal what is the fruit of your labor. I also broke down eight scenarios of what might have gradually drawn you or caused you to draw away from God.

You saw the process the old serpent used on Adam and Eve to deceive them and rob them of paradise and their relationship with God. It is in this way that Satan reveals his foundation for humanism through the lust of the flesh, the lust of the eyes, and a boastful pride of life, tricking millions into turning their backs on God. Satan will have you ask yourself, "Why isn't it okay if I take my new boat out on the lake and miss the Sunday worship service? Why can't I put myself first? Why do I have to give up my valuable time to help other people?"

I showed you Jesus teaching the rich young ruler who was doing everything right, according to the religious folk. The young ruler had not noticed his wealth becoming his god, and he then was unable to surrender that which he obviously worshipped. I discussed Jesus's parable of the seed thrown amongst the thorns and how this represented the cares of the world creeping into your life.

I will now bring you to the truth. At the beginning of this chapter I told you about a type of interrogation technique used to get a suspect to confess to the commission of a crime. I used this technique on you. You learned that many Christians allow humanism or "I" to creep into their lives and then turn their backs on God. You also saw how it is possible to get caught up into selfishness or humanism (the I factor) by examining the feelings that went along with each scenario. These simple thoughts give way to enthroning ourselves and our desires above God.

Finally, I asked you to identify with one of these scenarios and even gave you an "out" to save face—turning your back on God was not your fault, but Satan's. I intentionally walked you into a corner to make you take an honest look at yourself by coming face-to-face with the truth. An investigator knows an honest person will normally face the truth and admit to wrongdoing, but a narcissistic person (a lover-of-self) will never admit that he has done something wrong. What is the truth in your situation?

> **Is it really Satan's fault**
> **that we commit sin?**

Let me ask, is it really Satan's fault that we commit the sin of self-first, or is committing the sin just a foundational principle of selfish humanism (the I factor)? Adam and Eve tried the blame argument with God in Genesis 3:12–13, in which Adam blamed the woman God had given him as a wife, and Eve blamed the serpent who deceived her. Now this argument did not work on God in the Garden of Eden, and it will not hold water with God today, as we make our own choices every day in life.

You can try "worldly wisdom" to justify your self-first mind-set, as secular psychologists and the media teach that sin and bad decisions are not your fault. Distorters of truth know if they are going to totally pervert the morals of our society and turn people from God, they must begin with you. The plan is to cause a domino effect, as you as parents unknowingly distort the truth to your children and in turn, your children distort it with theirs. Do you see Satan's handiwork here?

Worldly wisdom unfortunately also finds its way into the Body of Christ. Paul warned the Galatians to be watchful of men creeping into the church to teach false doctrines, which were religious traditions and humanism. In Jude verse 4 we read, "For certain persons have crept in unnoticed, those who were long beforehand marked out for this condemnation, ungodly persons who turn the grace of our God into licentiousness and deny our only Master and Lord, Jesus Christ." Here stands a major problem for the Body of Christ, as liberal theologians and teachers have crept in to teach humanism and the lack of need for accountability. The result is good Christian people turning into self-loving people who often get offended when confronted with the truth of sin.

They leave the church instead of admitting that they put self-first before God. Liberal teachers have tried to convince you with a smile that if you will say a simple prayer you will have eternal life. This deception also involves preachers and teachers who are in love with the sound of their own voices and do not teach the deep messages of God, but who teach shallow messages that gradually starve believers. These teachers also proclaim there is no need to admit sin or ask for forgiveness or live a godly life, only admit Jesus is Lord. Have you had the wool pulled over your eyes?

The Bible, however, does not provide worldly wisdom but a "Godly wisdom," which teaches you must both confess your sins and have heartfelt repentance before you are forgiven. The Bible then teaches the forgiven to strive for a life for Christ. Paul writes in 1 Thessalonians 4:6–7, "For God has not called us for the purpose of impurity, but in sanctification. Consequently, he who rejects this is not rejecting man but the God who gives His Holy Spirit to you."

Where do you stand? Are you an honest person who can come face-to-face with the truth? Being honest, are you able to look inside your own heart? Can you stand up and admit that you have allowed self-interest, worldly lust for possessions or prestige, stagnation, the compromise of your values, or spiritual satisfaction to creep in and begin to control your life? Do you now understand why, even with all your toys, you have felt empty and unhappy and why there seems to be no purpose in your life? Do you understand why, when you are wrapped up in your own life, your flesh rises up any time you are asked to help others? Paul tells us in Romans 6:16, "Do you not know that when you present yourselves to someone as slaves for obedience, you are slaves of the one whom you obey, either of sin resulting in death, or of obedience resulting in righteousness?" With regard to self-interest, you cannot have it both ways: one foot in the world and one foot in God's Kingdom. You alone have to decide whom you will serve. So, if you are able to admit within your heart the sin of selfishness, then it is time to move forward. Therefore, I'm going to next discuss the olive principle and in the following chapters I will explain how you can learn how to once again reflect the glory of God on your face.

Chapter Four:
The Olive Principle

I told you back in chapter one that I lived in Italy, where my father served as a command sergeant major in the U.S. Army. We lived in a small village on the north side of Naples. It was a paradise of adventure for a kid who thought he was Huckleberry Finn. Other American military kids—my partners in crime—and I explored every orchard, grove, vineyard, cultivated terrace, and beach within our entire domain. If you can, imagine in your mind's eye this country, sitting right on the Mediterranean Sea, with remnants of World War II concrete weapon/machine gun bunkers, caves, and steep terraced hills, almost to the sea's edge. This was our playground.

While I explored the landscape, I also learned a lot about the culture by watching these ancient agricultural people of the former Roman Empire. The Italian farmers went about their daily lives: cultivating, pruning, and harvesting. I saw the devotion as the farmers worked every day to cultivate around their trees or vines, water when it was dry, and after the harvest, prune back their vines and trees in preparation for the next season. I watched as the farmers also went about picking grapes, apples, apricots, figs, and olives from their small orchards, groves, and vineyards scattered throughout the countryside. What I remember most is watching how the farmers, their wives, and children, as though in celebration, would use these long, cane-like poles to strike the branches of the trees to shake down the fruit. It appeared to be a long and tiring process in order to bring in a harvest, yet it was evidently a time-tested method that brought much success. My partners in crime and some of the Italian kids we played soccer with would wait until after dark and climb these small fruit trees to retrieve the fruit that refused to fall during the harvest. (Until we were discovered by the farmer.) As a child I was grateful some of the produce, whether figs, olives, or apricots, refused to release themselves to the harvesters.

I find it interesting how the Holy Spirit is able to bring back memories of things we have learned, apparently long-forgotten. While I was trying to understand what the Holy Spirit meant by the olive principle when He told me to write this book, He began to bring these childhood memories back to life. It amazes me that God in His great wisdom uses every little event from our lives to teach us a greater good to benefit His Kingdom and ourselves.

The olive tree (our lives) has a purpose and that is to bear fruit. When planted, the tree is placed in the ground and tenderly attended to. Growth is a process, so the soil is of great importance to the olive tree, as good fertile soil allows for a greater rate of growth. The farmer (God) cares for the young tree, planting it in His olive grove. The Farmer cultivates around the young tree, watering and providing nourishment so it has every advantage in its growth.

Cultivating requires the Farmer to keep weeds (concerns of life) away from the tree's roots so that it may receive water and nourishment. The Farmer takes great care in watering the olive tree, as without water the tree becomes weak and susceptible to disease. The water referred to here is the same as that referenced by Jesus when he spoke to the Samaritan woman: the continuous refreshing of the Holy Spirit through prayer and worship. Signs that a tree is not receiving water are that its leaves begin to turn yellow and brown; they then begin falling off the branches along with the fruit. In extreme cases of drought, the roots pull up to the surface. So it is with us that not drinking of the Holy Spirit, we begin to dry up spiritually. Exposure of the roots at the surface is a sign of starvation, and the tree in desperation reaches out for any nutrient or water that happens by. In us, the signs include not wanting to go to church or to take part in fellowship with our Christian brothers and sisters. In the case of starvation, we may fall away from God altogether.

Nourishment (the Word of God, preaching, and Christian fellowship) is directly provided by the Farmer, and it is the source of life-sustaining growth. Interestingly, while the tree is being fed on the surface, the real growth is taking place out of sight. The olive tree grows taller, and all the while the root system is keeping pace by growing wider and deeper, equaling the growth seen on the surface. This unseen growth is the constant inner work of the

Holy Spirit in our lives. The importance to the olive tree is that the roots' width and depth protect the tree from being blown over by storms or flash floods. They serve the same purpose in our walk, for when we are nourished with the Word of God and allow the Holy Spirit to work within our hearts, we develop an unyielding foundation of strength that can withstand the storms of life. The nourishment of the Word of God has a second part to play in the growth process, as the Word is like fertilizer with insecticide, which not only gives a boost in strength, but also protects the tree from within in order to withstand disease. If not constantly fed, the tree's growth is slowed, leaf blight disease and parasites may attack, and the promise of fruit lessened.

Now the farmer knows this tree is not going to bear fruit for some time, as you see fruit only comes through the process of maturity, which includes pruning. In pruning, the dead or unproductive areas of the tree are cut back, so that new growth will take place. In the spiritual sense, pruning is the process God uses (as the Greek word for pruning is translated) to cleanse or remove the unproductive parts of our lives and enable new growth.

With time the tree grows stronger and taller. Then, as it comes into its life purpose, it miraculously displays a few shining blossoms that may develop into ripe fruit. Although the young buds have not yet fulfilled their purpose, they are edible and can be used to sustain a hungry person coming to the tree for food. These buds (growing Christians) are intended to be used by the Holy Spirit, and they will bring divine appointments to feed someone or share the gospel with a hurting friend.

The maturing olive tree displays not a few blossoms, but blooms upon every branch and twig; and to the farmer's joy there are signs of olive fruit growing. The Farmer's family (Body of Christ) gathers around with encouragement and celebration as the fruit reaches its maximum weight, gently ripens, becomes plump, and signals the time of harvest is near. The Farmer is more diligent than ever in his watch over the tree and its fruit, to prevent defects from occurring in the final stages of the tree's growth. The defects God is watchful of are leaf blight disease and parasites (Satan's schemes or the results of the I factor) that attack the health of the olive tree and cause the fruit not to ripen properly or to die on the branch altogether.

Finally, the time arrives, and with great determination and celebration the farmer proceeds into the olive grove. The next stage includes shaking (ministry call) the ornamental-sized trees, so that the olives release themselves to the harvest and let go of the safety of the tree. The fruit of the farmer's labor is now gathered and with no time to spare is rushed off to the mill for processing.

After the long and burdensome growing process, the mill (olive press) is where the purpose of the olive fruit is revealed. The olives are first sorted according to size and weight, as only the plumpest olives are chosen to make oil. These olives are crushed, making a paste. The olive paste is then pressed without heat and releases its oil. Next the oil is cold-filtered to remove impurities and water (any distraction that might weigh us down) and quickly sent off for selection of grade. Why is the oil cold-filtered? John chapter 15 tells us that if we abide in Christ (stay rooted), then we are already clean from the Word (nourishment). This means that since you are already clean, your fruit will remain (be eternal) and therefore heating (testing) the ripe fruit is not required. Filtering is done to ensure that any unseen impurities are removed. The Oil Master (the Holy Spirit) then tastes the oil to find the top grade, and the rest is blended with other oils (others with gifting) to obtain different grades of olive oil for other purposes. All the oil, both the choicest and the blended grades selected by the Oil Master, are quickly packaged and sent around the world to benefit millions of people. But there is also the fruit that is ripened for a different purpose: as with the buds that are edible, the ripe fruit is packaged for the sole purpose of feeding the hungry.

In short, the process is as follows: God gives us life through receiving Jesus as our Savior and it is out of death (sin) that we are given the hope of eternal life. God plants us in fertile soil that promotes good growth on both the surface and inside our hearts. God cultivates, waters, nourishes, and prunes us through many different events (temporary in nature) and trials of our lives, to help us become who we are today. James 1:2–4 states, "Consider it all joy, my brethren when you encounter various trials, knowing that the testing of your faith produces endurance. And let endurance have its perfect result, that you may be perfect and complete, lacking in nothing." Dr. Larry Hunt writes in his book, *An Exposition of the Book of James*:

> Daily trials and situations will bring out of us [expose] that which is really there.

They provide a proving ground for our faith as to whether it is genuine or not. ...

...Therefore, because of our past life experiences with God, let us experientially know, let us perceive that these many-colored daily situations will, in fact, work out for our ultimate good and produce godly character in us. Eternal good will indeed come out of it.

You see, God uses any number of daily events, such as difficult situations at school or work, or financial problems, to perfect your faith and bring you to a place of maturity. Let us remember these situations are temporary and not permanent, unless we hold onto them and allow them to develop into sin. Remember how the farmer cultivated the young olive tree, which included watering it when it was dry, nourishing it when it needed to be fed, and pruning it when it needed to be cleansed of unproductive areas to enable growth. It is not until signs of maturity are present that the blossoms of fruit are detected.

> **The crushing and pressing must be voluntary in order for the choicest oil (gifting) to be obtained.**

As the tree matures, the true fruit begins to grow, and God continually checks the fruit to ensure it is growing both properly and without defect. God's continuous care and watchful eye are to guarantee that the fruit ripens for the very purpose it was created: to generate oil (gifting with purpose) or to feed the hungry (spiritual food). But, as you may recall, I mentioned earlier that there always seemed to be fruit that would not release itself to the harvest. The Holy Spirit showed me that this fruit represents the I factor, for it refuses to leave the safety of its comfort zone or self-loving interest. This is the fruit that unfortunately dries up on the branch and is of no use to the farmer. The ripe fruit, however, releases itself for the purpose that is programmed deep within its very DNA and joyfully submits to the next step of being crushed to release the oil (gifting) or to feed the needy (spiritual food). The crushing and pressing must be voluntary in order for the choicest oil (gifting) to be obtained. Luke 20:18 records Jesus's words, "Everyone who falls on that stone will be broken to pieces; but on whomever it falls, it will scatter him like dust." The word "fall," in the Greek, is an aorist participle, which is an action to take place at an undetermined time. In other words, the event of allowing yourself to be released or crushed in surrender to God's purpose will occur at a time set only for you. In this passage, the use of the word "fall" also means going from a higher to a lower standing with regard to a personal view of self. John the Baptist understood this, as he is recorded saying in John 3:30, "He must increase, but I must decrease." Jesus makes it very clear that the event of surrendering your will to Him is your choice and your choice alone, but if you refuse to surrender you will effectively die on the branch and not be used for the Kingdom of God. Matthew 7:7–8 says, "Every tree that does not bear good fruit is cut down and thrown into the fire. So then, you will know them by their fruits."

Therefore, in brief, the olive principle is:

- You were created to have a purpose in your physical and spiritual life.

- God uses the many temporary events in your life to promote growth (cultivating, watering, nourishing, and pruning) to bring you to a place of maturity.

- With maturity, the farmer is joyful to see us bearing fruit and he celebrates the harvest.

- After the harvest, the fruit will surrender itself to being crushed. In order to release the anointing (gifting with purpose) which has been developing within it, you must place your wants and desires second to God's desires.

- The oil (gifting) or fruit (spiritual food) is then ready to be sent all around the world with the farmer's label (the gospel of Jesus) on it to be used for the very purposes for which it was determined.

> ### Jesus had the example of surrender all around Him.

Jesus gave us the model for the olive principle. Jesus's life followed the process of the olive principle; He laid down His divine nature to become a common man. Jesus would allow God to cultivate, water, nourish, and prune Him if necessary. Jesus allowed God to watch over Him while blight and parasites (Satan's schemes) lurked nearby. Jesus understood that the fruit He was to bear would bring the choicest oil (gift) and fruit (spiritual food) of all—salvation for all mankind.

The final step of the olive principle, crushing, can be found in Luke 22:39–46. In this passage, Jesus climbs to the Garden of Gethsemane on the Mount of Olives in order to seek His Father before laying down His life for you and me. It is fitting that the Garden of Gethsemane (olive press) was the location Jesus Himself chose to teach us about laying down our will to the Father. Jesus understood His "self-will" must be crushed in order for the gift of salvation to flow forth and for there to be success of the Father's eternal purpose. Jesus prayed in verse 42, "Father, if Thou are willing, remove this cup from Me; yet not My will, but Thine be done." I hear Jesus's thoughts loud and clear to God: "What you are asking me to do (be a missionary, serve in children's ministry, be a mentor to a new Christian) is hard, but Your will, or the choicest oil (greatest gift) is more important than my will."

Luke gives us the full effect of the crushing process where he continues in verse 44, "And being in agony He was praying fervently and His sweat became like drops of blood, falling down to the ground." Jesus understood that in order for Him to fulfill His calling, the process would be hard, as He (the Son of God) would be humiliated (the Son-of-God). Jesus would be spat upon, beaten with fists, and scourged with pieces of metal. His flesh and bones would be ripped, He would be nailed to a cross, and He would take on (all) the sin of the world. But the worst part for Jesus would be that His Father would turn His back on Him and allow Jesus to die. Jesus agonized to the point of physical collapse, and the Bible tells us His sweat was [like] drops of blood. I heard a medical professional state that the only way someone could sweat blood would be if he were under overwhelming emotional distress, causing the capillaries in his face to burst. The blood from the capillaries would then flow into the sweat ducts and emerge as droplets of blood. Can you imagine being under such overwhelming stress that your capillaries burst? With my limited human mind, I can only try to imagine the extent of Jesus's emotional stress (crushing). An example of lesser proportion, yet earthshaking for a parent, would be to have your child dying on a hospital bed, and learning from the doctor there is nothing more he could do, so you had better pray. How intense would your prayer to the Father be, knowing that you needed God to hear you? Jesus had the example of surrender all around Him in the Garden of Gethsemane, as He knew that just like Him, the olives growing in the trees would have to be crushed in order to fulfill the purpose for which God intended. Are you willing to climb to the Garden of Gethsemane?

The Bible gives us other examples of men who went through the olive principle process and came to see the big picture modeled by Jesus. This is the process that you must go through. To help you along the path, in the next chapter I will provide a couple of character studies of people just like you and me, who came to understand the olive principle and the oil produced by being crushed.

Chapter Five:
A Murderer and a Brawler

The character studies I will now discuss are about two ordinary men living out what they believed were godly lives. Each had his own personal struggle in coming to understand the olive principle. Each had to come to grips with how he must go through the process of the olive tree and make the choice to surrender his will to God in order to produce fruit and oil.

First I will look at the story of the shepherd boy–warrior–fugitive–king in David, a man with a checkered past. Most teachers spend a great deal of time reflecting on David's slaying Goliath, his writing many of the Psalms, and his desire to build a temple for God. Even beyond those achievements, David was a complex character who went through many circumstances to arrive at the point of surrendering to being crushed so the gift of leadership could emerge in his life.

We first notice David when he was a teenager out herding and protecting sheep (1 Samuel 16:11). It was during this part of David's life that he was planted in fertile soil for God's purpose. David was cultivated and watered in the process by receiving the foundational knowledge of the Word of God from his father Jesse, and also by learning how to care for (lead) his father's flock. David was taught by his father where to graze the sheep, where to find fresh water for them to drink, and where to position himself (roots deep and wide) to ward off an attack by a wild beast. I do not know whether David realized it, but he was also learning to build an intimate relationship with God while praying and worshiping. His prayers and worship allowed the inner working of the Holy Spirit into his life. David understood at an early age how to be alone with God and experience His divine presence in his life. It is also in this early stage that David was selected by God to be a leader, anointed by Samuel to be the next king of Israel.

> **David proved not only was the Word of God firmly planted within his heart, but the faith in his life brought victory in battle.**

We actually get to know young David on the battlefield. Even in his youth, David ran into battle against the Philistines, who were the longtime enemy of Israel. David was chosen by God to destroy a giant; however, this was not any old giant, but one that brought fear and destruction to the entire nation of Israel. The young warrior did realize he had the weapon with which to go forth and destroy Goliath (unfortunately many teachers make the mistake of only looking at the slingshot and smooth stones, and ignore the true weapon of that battle). As David ran out to meet Goliath, he cried, "You come to me with a sword, a spear, and a javelin, but I come to you in the name of the Lord of hosts, the God of the armies of Israel, whom you have taunted" (1 Samuel 17:45). David proved not only was the Word of God firmly planted within his heart, but also the roots of faith ran wide and deep in his life, and brought victory in battle.

We fast-forward to 1 Samuel 22, in which David took refuge from King Saul in the Cave of Adullam. It was here that David's family fled to him, along with every other oppressed and downtrodden person running from this self-serving king. It was there on the run from King Saul that God began the pruning process in David's life. Pruning taught David to trust God as his supplier and allowed God, through daily circumstances, to develop the gift of leadership inside David. David led a ragtag group of four hundred men. His story reminds me of one of my favorite war movies, *The Dirty Dozen*. In the movie, actor Lee Marvin takes a handful of misfits who are locked in jail and turns them into an elite fighting force used to destroy a German fortress during World War II. This is exactly what David did; he took downtrodden people from the lower class that no one else wanted, met their needs, encouraged them, and turned them into an elite force—later known as David's mighty men of valor. This is an example of the olive principle: David's men were the growing buds that provided fruit for those who were hungry.

David's elite force of gifted warriors, who could fight with either hand, were able to use multiple weapons. They were fearless in nature. The growth in David and his men was the outward manifestation of the inward working of the Holy Spirit, so as storms arose David could continue to move forward (not retreat) and fight even when wounded. David's growth began to produce fruit, as skilled men were not only trained to defeat the enemy, but were themselves taught to bear fruit modeled by their leader. David encountered and sheltered both the poor and the wealthy, both laborers and professionals, and devoted citizens as well as former convicts. But what impresses me is how David allowed the source of his strength to feed others and advance the Kingdom of God. David's example of God's love served as the foundation of his relationship of trust with others and allowed him to lead them into fulfilling God's purpose.

We move forward to the point further in 2 Samuel where David had established himself as king. But it was not pie-in-the-sky for David from there on out. As the king, he pulled away from His source and encountered blight and parasites in his growth cycle. First, David blew it when he decided to move the Ark of the Covenant in a manner fitting his agenda and different from that of God's will. Once David repented and yielded to God's will, the Ark was moved successfully to Jerusalem, and there God made a new covenant with him. Next, we find in chapter 11 that David fell for the lust of eyes and of the flesh in desiring the beautiful Bathsheba, and after falling into the sin of adultery, he conspired in his heart to commit murder. David actually sent Bathsheba's husband, Uriah, on a suicide assault against a stronghold of the Ammonites at Rabbah and had his general Joab withdraw the forces to allow Uriah to be killed. If this is not a clear demonstration of the I factor, then I do not know what is. God would send his prophet to pronounce judgment on David's sin, and once again came both repentance and restoration. David had pulled away and then remembered his spiritual roots.

There are other events attributed to David's lack of judgment and not staying under the Farmer's (God's) care that brought problems to him and the nation of Israel, but he was quick to repent and learn from his mistakes. It is these temporary circumstances and pruning in David's life that brought him to submit to his cleansing himself of distractions and the results of the I factor. The Bible says that God forgave David and continued to use this imperfect man to bear much fruit in order to advance His Kingdom. Is there a lesson for us here?

The final character I will briefly study was a tough sort of man's man and one who does not impress me as a person who on a normal day would have walked away from a fight. When I think of an individual like this I am drawn to those hardened by the sea, like the commercial fishermen you see on the show, *The Deadliest Catch.* You know the type: hardheaded, rough-talking, with no real fear of the elements, and personalities molded by the physical demands of their work. With this type of man in mind, we meet Simon, called Peter in Matthew 4:18–20, who was selected by Jesus to come and follow Him and become a fisher of men.

To understand Peter, we need a quick review of Jewish tradition and life. Peter came from a traditional Jewish background, where most were involved in agricultural work. The Jews held to the law of Moses, the prophets, and established traditions. The story of Peter is another example of God planting someone in fertile soil so rapid growth could take place. Peter was called by Jesus to come and follow Him in ministry and be a fisher of men.

During this period of time, becoming a disciple (learner) meant leaving your family and work to follow a teacher, as Peter was set aside for God's olive grove and a divine purpose. Here we see the development of Peter, and that his process of cultivation and watering was more intense than that of others. He was like the hybrid olive tree that must grow quickly and begin bearing fruit in a shorter time span. We follow Jesus's ministry, and it becomes apparent His focus was on preparing the twelve disciples by demonstrating biblical principles in daily events around them (such as miracles or healing). Jesus would then call the disciples aside to give them spiritual understanding (nourishment for root growth) for future use. I could spend pages discussing Jesus's model of training, but I will refer you to Robert E. Coleman's classic: *The Master Plan of Evangelism.* This is a small book that I sat down and read in one day, and it has become a permanent and important part of my personal library.

> **Jesus purposely walked across the water to provoke pruning in Peter's life.**

Jesus understood that He only had a brief time to train Peter and the other disciples, so he poured on the Miracle-Gro of nourishing. In Peter's life, pruning involved failures so that the workings of the Holy Spirit could bring change into his life.

Let us fast-forward to Matthew 14:22–33, in which Jesus had just fed the five thousand and sent the disciples ahead so He could have a quiet time with God. I believe Jesus purposely walked across the water to provoke pruning—not only for Peter, but also for the rest of the disciples. Jesus called Peter out of his comfort zone and asked him to trust in Him. You will remember the boat kept Peter safe from the fury of the crashing sea around him, just as an olive clings to a branch. Peter had to learn to trust the Lord and stay focused (rooted) on his source. Possibly, Peter got caught up in the I factor, becoming overconfident and (perhaps wanting to make sure the others were watching) his pride averted his eyes from the source of his strength. (I look at this story through my lens of having dealt with self-confident cops.) The result was falling into a dangerous and self-created problem, in which weeds and "self" blinded him. But once Peter refocused his eyes on the Lord, there was a hand to lift him up. There also seems to be a lesson to learn here.

Peter was focused on who Jesus was as stated in Matthew 16:16, "Thou are the Christ, the Son of the living God," and he displayed the signs of actual olive fruit beginning to bud out and grow in his life. We must understand that Peter is like many of us who do not always get it. For example, in Matthew 16:21–23 we see Jesus foretelling His death, and the hardheaded Peter rebuking the Lord for such a thought. Peter, although beginning to grow fruit, displayed the strong need for the Farmer (God) to protect him from blight and parasites, as he allowed Satan's worldly wisdom to surface in his life. However, in Matthew 17:1–8 Jesus takes Peter, James, and John with Him and is transfigured before them. Now this would definitely be a life-changing event for anyone. I believe that at this moment Peter understood Jesus was the long-awaited Jewish messiah, yet we see through continuous lessons and parables that Peter and the other disciples needed further nourishing and pruning. Growth is a process.

Again, we fast-forward for the sake of brevity to the Last Supper, at which Jesus announced one among them would betray Him. I believe that there in that moment the brawler (the fleshly self) in Peter surfaced again. He wanted to know whom this person was, as he was going to bring some accountability to the situation. Peter's personality showed that there were still impurities within him that could hinder or cause defect in the proper ripening of the fruit in his life. We see this "self" again when Peter flatly denied he would desert Jesus in His time of need, and finally when, without thinking, he drew a sword in defense of God in the flesh.

Matthew 18:25–27 reminds us of Peter's denial of Jesus to the world, which I believe was a pivotal moment in his life and the point where he was being harvested by the Farmer (God). After some soul searching and probably surrendering to being crushed (olive press), Peter emerged from the shadows not as the brawler, but as a leader (gifting with purpose) among the other disciples. And after receiving the power of the Holy Spirit on the day of Pentecost, Peter went forth and worked tirelessly, bearing much fruit, for the Kingdom of God. Did Peter still make mistakes? Yes, but it appears clear throughout the book of Acts that Peter submitted to the Oil Master (Holy Spirit), surrendered his will, and was used to reach hundreds if not thousands of both Jews and gentiles because of it. Finally, if you want to see the difference between Peter as a young olive tree and a mature, deeply rooted tree, just take some time to study the books of 1 and 2 Peter.

I want to take a moment and give a heartfelt explanation at this point. I am not in any way attempting to demean these previous two heroes of the Bible. I recognize, as you do, that God Himself called these men for His sovereign purpose, to which I submit. The purpose of these stories is to show how the olive principle was displayed in regular, imperfect people just like you and me. Furthermore, God has been faithful to us in making His Word totally transparent by showing that none of us is perfect and without weakness in our lives. The Holy Spirit inspired Paul to record in Romans 3:23 that "all have sinned and fall short of the glory of God" and again in 1 John 1:8, "If we say that we have no sin we are deceiving ourselves, and the truth is not in us."

The studies show each of us God's desire to use regular, everyday, imperfect human beings by planting us in fertile ground. God will cultivate, water, nourish, and prune us to promote growth. God furthermore puts us on a path of maturity to grow strong roots to withstand the storms of life, bear much fruit, and willingly lay down our self-interest and the rest of our lives (oil press) for the purpose He has gifted us.

I am of the opinion that many times we view these characters in the Bible as bigger than life. Maybe this misunderstanding occurs because the way the information is presented in children's church and by many pastors. Whatever the reason, we often do not believe God could ever use people like you and me in such a great way. This is in fact the path that God wants us to travel. Therefore, in the next chapter, I will discuss the trail back to God's will.

Chapter Six:
Take the Worn Trail

I remember while growing up on army bases how my fellow junior GI Joes and I would go out in search of our next great adventure. One time that stands out is when my father came back from Vietnam and was stationed at Fort Leonard Wood, Missouri, in the heart of the Mark Twain National Forest. My friends and I would search for trails that the basic training soldiers used and noticed how these trails were always worn down from the hundreds of soldiers who had marched along before us. Have you ever been to a state or national park and started up one of those "marked" trails? If so, did you see the way in which the trail was worn down into the earth by the hundreds (if not thousands) who had be there before you? There were signs warning you to stay on the marked trails for your own safety, as the marked trail was a proven way to get to your desired designation. So it is with the worn and proven trail taken by thousands before you from the place of sin and self-first back to the place of promise and God's olive grove. Join me in walking this worn trail as I compare an historical journey from the Old Testament with a believer's journey back to God.

In Genesis 47, we find that Joseph has brought his family (Israel) into the green and fertile land of Goshen in Egypt, where they flourish and grow with prosperity. This story can be likened to our pursuit of the American dream of a beautiful home and a nice automobile—in other words, enjoying the fat (toys) of our personal achievements. The olive tree (you) are enjoying the benefits of fertile soil. However, for some, a change begins to take place, as described in Exodus 1:7–14—the personal achievements of Israel opened it up to the rule of a new king. This king placed the people into bondage and put taskmasters over them, forcing the people into a life of hard labor. In our lives, we feel blessed, and we are on top of the world, but Satan's plan is to entice us into the lust of the eyes, the lust of the flesh, and the pride of life. (We discover weeds begin to spring up around us.) Now instead of feeling joy from being blessed by God and finding success in the world, you find yourself enslaved to a large mortgage payment, having to have that new car to one-better your friends, and keeping up with the Joneses by buying your kids the latest iPad or the exclusive and highly-priced sports gear. At this point in the developing humanistic walk (the I factor), there is worry over finances, which causes joy to exit from your life, leaving only a type of hollow and unfulfilling existence in search of personal significance. This is the olive tree (you) being caught up in life, but not wanting the Farmer (God) to cultivate, water, and nourish in order to keep the weeds (I factor) away from your roots. Without water, the olive tree begins to weaken and has difficulty in receiving the life-sustaining nourishment.

We now find in Exodus 2:23–25 the Israelites groaning under the weight of Egypt's bondage, and they began to cry out to God for deliverance. I believe this is a turning point for a lot of people, myself included. Having become a slave to your possessions and the need for more, you may come to grips with how miserable your life is and begin to cry out for relief. The Holy Spirit hears you. The Farmer (God) sees that His olive tree is engulfed in weeds and knows that soon blight and parasites will attack and begin to drain the life out of this precious tree. If asked, the Farmer will come quickly to bring healing.

In Exodus chapter 3, we see Moses receives his call at the burning bush, and God's redemptive plan is moved into action. This plan of redemption is the same for us—even before the beginning of time, God the Father, God the Son, and God the Holy Spirit had a corporate meeting, and the Son dedicated Himself to paying the price of the redeemer for you. Do you realize that if you were the only person in sin on the earth, Jesus would have offered to come and die for you?

Continuing in Exodus chapters 4 through 12, we see that God sent Moses into Egypt to deliver the people out of the bondage of slavery. Moses, as the chosen redeemer of Israel, went to the people and informed them that God was going to deliver them. The king of bondage recognized the plan and tightened his grip. By doing so, he induced more pain, causing the people to stop their struggle and settle back into slavery. (Blight and parasites dig in deep in their mission to destroy.) Through the process of the ten plagues (the manifested power of God through miracles), the king of bondage loosened his grip. There was yet one important step for Israel to take in order to be free, and this was taking part in the slaying of the lamb as read in Exodus chapter 12. It is only through the drawing of the Spirit of God that you can be redeemed and forgiven by Jesus Christ, but for many this is when the real struggle begins. The olive tree must plunge its roots in the source of nourishment in order to have the ability to become healthy once more. I remember when I was crying out to God to help me; something was tearing at me and I experienced attack after attack in every area of my life. I found in my experience with some people that when some effort brings great pain, we tend to set it aside. I find it awesome that God knows how to manifest Himself to us in unique ways so as to convince us He is for real, just as He did through the miracles and plagues for Israel. God will provide the insecticide within prayer and the Word to bring an end to disease. For you, however, just as for Israel, there cannot be redemption from the grips of bondage until you first take part in the blood of the sacrificed Lamb of God. It is only by coming to the place of heartfelt repentance (allowing God to cultivate you), that you are allowed to confess your sin and be spiritually washed by the blood of Christ.

> **The devil has been defeated and can no longer forcibly take you hostage against your will.**

With the redemption of the Passover lamb, Moses lead Israel out of Egypt and toward the Red Sea, and there God peeled back the waters and allowed Israel to walk through dry and untouched. All the while the king of bondage was in hot pursuit, willing to sacrifice thousands of his own to bring death to those he hated. God was on His game and prepared for the enemy's charge, bringing down tons of water to close the door He opened and completing the victory. I want you to understand that just because you decide to return to God through repentance, it does not mean the devil is going to give up. Because you were created in God's image, and he hates God, the devil hates you. His every action is a continuous act of revenge. The Farmer (God) knowing the devil's plan made a way for you through the blood of His son Jesus. The blood gives you victory over the devil. Just as pharaoh stood looking in defeat, so the devil stands looking at you in defeat. Did you understand what I said? The devil has been defeated and can no longer forcibly take you hostage against your will.

We see in Exodus chapter 15 that when they realized they were free from slavery, Israel began to sing what was named the "Song of Moses." This was a time of great rejoicing and the women danced before the Lord, praising Him for their deliverance. This time of rejoicing is the same in the olive principle, where every branch and twig bursts out in blooms. There is a joy in the kingdom for the revived olive tree.

In the last part of Exodus chapter 15 and through the first half of chapter 17, we see Israel has entered the wilderness and has begun to thirst and hunger for spiritual water and the Word. Of course, being new to this experience, they were as little children—

still filled with worldly attitudes (remains of the I factor) and thinking only of their own needs. It is God who displays patience and provides water for them, then manna, and finally meat, in order to bring the people along to a different place. It is also at this point that the Farmer is able to cultivate around the tree, and then it will receive much-needed water and nourishment. When you have fallen into sin and then return to Christ, there is refreshment, but work begins in the wilderness. The work of the wilderness is the pruning process, where the Farmer (God) begins to cut away the worldly cares and major impurities in the olive tree's life. Those who have fallen away reek of worldly attitudes (I factor) and their first thought is to take care of their own needs. The pruning process is explained by Paul in Ephesians 4:22–24: "In reference to your former manner of life, you lay aside the old self, which is being corrupted in accordance with the lusts of deceit, and that you be renewed in the spirit of your mind, and put on the new self, which is in the likeness of God has been created in righteousness and holiness of truth." Paul was talking about undressing yourself or pruning away worldly attitudes and then redressing yourself with an outfit of right living (wanting blight and parasites removed) before God. It is also here in the wilderness where God pours on the attention in you through preachers and other Christians, so you will draw near to Him. God uses this renewed desire for growth to draw you into His Word (nourishment) in order to give you some meat to gnaw on and help the process of maturity to begin. The wilderness is also the place of learning how to allow the inward working of the

Holy Spirit to again have charge of your life (roots growing wide and deep).

While in the wilderness, Israel was led to Mount Sinai (Exodus 19), and God drew the people aside to a place where He could build a personal relationship with them. Mount Sinai is the place where God wanted to write His law into the hearts of the people and teach them how to maintain this newfound love relationship. The olive tree reaches its branches to the heavens in worship. It was also the place where the people of Israel would have to decide whether they would begin to produce fruit or fall back into idol worship where there is only certain death. I personally think this is the place from which some people never advance; for some, when God begins to make Himself real to them, it is so overwhelming that they turn their faces away as Israel did. You see, when God is making Himself real to you, there is the knowledge inside your heart that there needs to be hard pruning. The problem with hard pruning is that the desires of "I" come into play, wanting it both ways—both to serve God and to hold on to your humanistic ways. This is like many of the Israelites who had Aaron build the golden calf to worship, as they wanted to hold on to the idols of bondage that satisfied the flesh. Whether you are turning to God for the first time, or are someone who knows God but has fallen into humanism once again, this is the place of decision. God loves you, and since He made you a creature of self-will, He will not force you to submit to pruning. You get to decide whether to spend eternity in heaven or hell. Fortunately, most people choose as Moses and the Levites did, and they destroy the things of the old life and follow the true God.

For forty years Israel wandered, wearing down a trail in the place of survival as seen in the remainder of the book of Exodus, and in the books of Leviticus and Numbers. This dilemma was a result of God's trying to lead Israel into the place of great abundance, but they feared what was before them (the olive that clings to the branch). Yet, God in His faithfulness used this time to teach the people how to spend time with Him, learn His ways, learn the discipline of obedience, learn to trust Him as their provider, and ultimately how to bear much fruit to draw all men to Him. Again, I am saddened by how many people I have met, who once lived for Christ as their Savior, but turned away and refused to submit to the process. It seems when the Holy Spirit began to prune them in order to stimulate growth or encourage the conforming of their minds, they pulled away from Him. I am unable to fully understand why some good and loving people seem to prefer to wander in the wilderness their whole lives instead of willingly yielding their will (self) to God's plan. [Please read Jeremiah 29:11–14.]

As we read in the book of Joshua, the next step for Israel was to cross the Jordan River and enter the land of Canaan. God had already led Israel to the Jordan once before, but as you remember from your studies, they refused to face what was before them, as there were giants occupying the new land. This time we discover God has a people who are willing to follow Him anywhere (the maturing olive tree), for this time the spies go into the land to study it and look for weakness in the enemy's camp. The spies already know about the giants to be fought (temporary circumstances of life), but this time they are on the offensive. For you this is where your roots are growing wide and deep. God would again peel back the water (Jordan River) and make a way for Israel to follow Him into a new place.

The Jordan River was to be the place of circumcision for Israel. For you today, the Jordan River is where God desires to lead you into a place of maturity and fruit-bearing, so His power can be manifested to the world through you. The Jordan River is the place where you are harvested; it is the place where you arrive after you have been watered, nourished, and pruned. It is the place for which the very purpose of the olive was created: it is the olive principle. You can go no further in reaching the planned fulfillment without surrendering "self" to God and stepping into the role for the Kingdom.

Joshua, chapter 6, describes the conquest of Canaan for the people of Israel. This possessing of territory involves overcoming giants, and battles to wage against strongholds. The process of dealing with overcoming giants in your life and battles fought brings maturity. This is the purpose of the olive tree having roots wide and deep—to withstand the storms and floods of life. Joshua was promised by the Lord that He would go before him and defeat the enemy (blight and parasites), if Israel would follow His instruction. Today the Lord leads us to the place of maturity where we are to bear much fruit, submit to the olive press, and take possession of the promises (gifting used in ministry) in His Word. Yes, there are going to be giants to overcome, and there are going to be battles to wage, as you cannot possess without conquering. You still have to battle your flesh; the enemy still wants to find a way to draw you back into a place of bondage. You are going to get a bruise and a scrape here and there, as this is the nature of warfare. Jesus never promised a pie-in-the-sky process, but told us in John 16:33, "In the world you have tribulation, but take courage; I have overcome the world." (That is the point so many miss; I cheated and read the end of the book—God wins!)

If you continue to follow the history of Israel, there are battles won and battles lost. You find there are times when the people of Israel again find themselves enslaved, redeemed, and enslaved, as with the seven cycles recorded in the book of Judges. There is a reoccurring theme: every time the people took their eyes off the source (God), they fell into sin (blight and parasites), and were taken into bondage (I factor). But, when Israel again had heartfelt repentance and cried out to God, they were forgiven, restored, and took possession of the land. As with other Christians today, as long as you are focused on God, you grow and bear fruit. Has this been a reoccurring theme for you? However, as soon as you took your eyes off your source—becoming self-satisfied, or willingly listening to the devil and pursuing the lust of the eyes, lust of the flesh, and pride of life, you were once again taken into bondage. Did you forget your first love? The Lord Jesus Christ stands waiting to give you a hand up out of bondage and emptiness. So what will you do? Read Revelation 3:20, then join me in the next chapter to find our way home.

Chapter Seven:
The Way to He, Not Me

In *The Olive Principle* we have taken a journey together, remembering what it was like when we first came to know Jesus as our personal Lord and Savior. Remember how you always had a smile on your face, you wanted to tell everyone about this Jesus, and you could simply not get enough of Him? Second, we took a look at the I factor or putting our desires first before putting ourselves out. We saw how the devil used the lust of the eyes, the lust of the flesh, and pride of life to deceive Adam and Eve, and how he has been using the same method throughout history in different forms of humanism. With humanism (self-love without accountability) being allowed within the Body of Christ, we have now created spiritual cripples. Third, we examined the fact that most of us have allowed ourselves at some point to become the center of our own universe, placing God in a secondary role. Fourth, we looked at the olive principle—the process in which

God develops us and the reason that we must allow our self-will to be crushed. Fifth, we did character studies of David and Peter to help see God's use of the olive principle, and how He takes regular, imperfect people like each of us through the process to advance the Kingdom. Sixth, we compared the nation of Israel with our modern lives. The reoccurring trail will always lead back to God. Through heartfelt repentance and the surrendering of self to His will, we are brought to a place of maturity and bearing of fruit.

One main point of this journey is to help those who have allowed themselves to be snared by the cares of this world. Being caught in a snare causes the fruit cultivated by God to become self-serving and literally die on the branch. Therefore, before I walk you through what are possibly some of the hardest steps you will ever have to take, let me first explain a purpose the Holy Spirit has put inside my heart. I refer you to Acts 3:1–7, in which Luke records the story of a cripple sitting daily by the temple gate begging for handouts. Peter, I believe led by the Holy Spirit, approached the man and looked at him; the man in a normal (spiritual cripple) fashion, expected his needs to be taken care of. However, Peter did not offer the man a reward for being a spiritual cripple, but instead offered him a hand out of his situation. To offer you a method out of your situation is the true reason the Holy Spirit told me to write *The Olive Principle.* Unfortunately, some pastors spend all their time babying Christians and catering to their selfish needs, rather than standing firm, calling sin sin, and offering them a hand up. I am not good at sugarcoating the truth, and I speak this in love—if you, as a Christian, have allowed yourself to be caught up in "self," then you are in sin. Now, I am here to offer you a hand up out of sin and to show you how to return to the olive grove and God's plan for you to bear much fruit. If you want this then we have work to do, but if you are offended, you have the right to choose and go back to your empty, unfulfilling, and unfruitful life.

First, if your heart has been aching because you know you are not right with God, you need to immediately go to a quiet place, confess your sin, and ask in the name of Jesus for God to forgive you. I am talking about that heartfelt, gut-wrenching repentance in which you know you are guilty before your Creator. 1 John 1:8 tells us, "If we confess our sin, He is faithful and righteous to forgive us our sins and to cleanse us from all unrighteousness." In layman terms, this means that if you go before God and admit you have sinned, He promises to do the right thing and forgive you. This means the sin is erased and no longer exists in the mind of God, and the Holy Spirit will help you to remove from your life the desire for sin. Luke also writes in 3:19, "Repent therefore and return, that your sins may be wiped away, in order for times of refreshing may come from the presence of the Lord." When you humble yourself before God, not only does He forgive you, but He begins to cultivate your life. I do not care what the sin is—murder, adultery, stealing or greed, alcohol or drugs, holding a grudge, abusing your spouse, selfishness—God does not see different levels of sin, He only sees sin. A dear friend and professor Andy Stump told me, "You need to keep a short account with God." Go ahead, confess to God and then we can continue.

Did you remember to thank God for His forgiveness? Remember we are to give thanks for all things. Go ahead and thank the Father who is always ready to forgive us, seventy times seventy, for our sin.

Now, I want you to give *your word* that five days a week you are going to set aside time (quiet time) to spend just with Him. Now I know you are already objecting by asking, "Do you know I hit the ground running every day?" Yes, and I also know that this is the first step in allowing God to begin the cultivation process.

> **Worship God by closing your eyes and proclaiming how much you love Him.**

- Start out with fifteen minutes a day. Start, for example, reading a chapter like John 10 each of the following five days: Monday, Tuesday, Thursday, Friday, and Saturday. This activity should only take you part of the fifteen minutes. Buy a bible concordance to look up the definition of words and discover what a verse is really saying. Pray before you open your Bible and ask the Holy Spirit to teach you, as He is the one who dictated it to the authors. Then read the Word, receive the Word into your soul (mind) and heart (spirit), and apply the Word to your life. James 1:22 says you must "prove yourselves doers of the word, and not merely hearers who delude themselves."

Teach yourself how to feed on the Word and if this seems difficult, then buy Kay Arthur's book, *How To Study Your Bible*. When you learn how to study, you will become hungry for God's Word! If you are starving, then it is imperative that you find a church that offers solid biblical teaching and not just mundane uninspired preaching. The study of God's Word is the nourishing stage of the olive principle, it keeps you rooted in the source of life. Fifteen minutes a day may not seem like a lot to some, but it is like exercise, you start out slowly and build up your strength. I purchased an elliptical machine for our home and although my wife warned me to take it slowly, I got rather cocky and within a few short minutes my legs were like rubber. The next time I started out at a lesser resistance, and I've gradually built up the difficulty. I will continue to build muscle (endurance) and reach my goal. If you try to do too much at one time, you stand a strong chance of becoming discouraged with your progress, and it's more than likely you'll stop. Building slowly will build muscle in your desire to spend time with God, and you will gradually begin setting more and more time aside for Him, allowing your roots to grow wide and deep.

- Take the rest of the time to pray. Prayer is easy; it is just talking to God like you would to your best friend. Then listen. Jeremiah 33:3 says, "Call to Me, and I will answer you, and I will tell you great and unsearchable things, which you do not know." Prayer is the foundation of Christian life—staying in relationship with God. Do you know how to pray? If you said no, then go to a prayer meeting or two and watch who is powerful in this area and ask the person to teach you. The Bible tells us Jesus often went to lonely places to pray and be with the Father; if Jesus, who was God in the flesh, needed this experience, don't you suppose we do? Having a quiet time with God is allowing the mirror of His Word, and the time alone with Him in prayer opens you to the intrinsic (inward) working of the Holy Spirit, so you may bear much fruit. Prayer is the watering process through which the continuous refreshing of the Holy Spirit is allowed to flow through your spirit.

- Worship God. Close your eyes and proclaim how much you love Him. Draw close to the one you love and allow the love inside you to flow out to your Creator and Master. The olive tree reaches its branches toward heaven in celebration of life, and the people rejoiced in Jesus's triumphal entry into Jerusalem. Luke 19:40 records Jesus's words: "And He answered and said, 'I tell you, if these become silent, the stones will cry out.'" How much more should our hearts cry out in love for our redeemer? Worship is also part of the watering process, and it allows communion with God.

- Keep a journal of what jumps out at you in your study time. Record both what you asked the Father for and what He may have spoke to you. I personally know that journaling is not for everyone, and there are conflicting opinions about whether this practice is effective. You must pray for guidance and make your own choice.

- Next, you need to find someone who will hold you accountable for remaining committed to the things of God, and to give him permission to speak (with love) into your life. I am talking about somebody who is a mature Christian, and who has a reputation for being trustworthy and for keeping his lips sealed. My wife and I are fortunate to be friends with a couple at our church to whom we are able to tell our deepest hurts and darkest secrets. They would rather be tortured than break our trust. They also check in with us to see what is going on in our physical and spiritual lives. Paul wrote in Colossians 2:5, "For even though I am absent in body, nevertheless I am with you in spirit, rejoicing to see your good discipline and the stability of your faith in Christ." Although Paul was writing to the Colossians about the supremacy of Christ, he took a moment to remind them he was keeping a check on how they were walking in Christ. Remember that the olive tree was checked on for its progress in growth and how the fruit was maturing. Weeds, blight, and parasites will try to creep in and slow growth or bring disease (sin) if not watched closely. I know, I know, this is going to be hard for some of you; it was difficult for me being a self-reliant old cop, but I actually like it now.

Don't run from God's pruning.

- Don't run from God's pruning. Recall from chapter four that the Farmer prunes the olive tree when He sees there is a need for new growth. I worked at a plant nursery for several years as a second job while a police officer. The first rule of plant care: if you want better growth, bigger blooms, or more fruit, you prune the plant hard. When preparing flats of petunias, or another flowering plant (like mums for a wedding or some type of festival), we would prune back the plants almost to the bare stem. Although we would lose a week's growth, the plants would come back stronger and generate masses of blooms. "Every branch that bears fruit, He prunes it, that it may bear more fruit" (John 15:2). An example of one who understood this principle after meeting Christ is Paul, who writes in Philippians 3:7–8:

> But whatever things were gain to me, those things I have counted as loss for the sake of Christ. More than that, I count all things to be loss in view of the surpassing value of knowing Christ Jesus my Lord, for whom I have suffered the loss of all things, and count them but rubbish in order that I may gain Christ.

And in verse 15, Paul further writes, "Let us therefore, as many as are perfect, have this attitude; and if in anything God will reveal that also to you." When God sees areas of your life that have impurities or are unproductive, He will, because He loves you, prune back your life hard to enable new growth and allow you to bear much fruit. Pruning is done in love and therefore must be received willingly in love.

• The next discipline is to focus on the things of God. Paul wrote in Colossians 3:1–2, "If then you have been raised up with Christ, keep seeking the things above, where Christ is, seated at the right hand of God. Set your mind on the things above, not on the things that are on earth." Remember that the devil hates you, and he is not done trying to trip you up. So although he cannot read your mind, he can try to cross your path with things you have trouble fighting. James 1:14–15 tells us that we are tempted when carried off and enticed by our own desires. Simply put, when we see something we have battled before and allow the image to take hold in our brain, we are then enticed, and we may allow the desire to grow. Our own desires—lust of the eyes, lust of the flesh, and the pride of life—literally take us in tow. In a lecture given by Dr. Larry Hunt, Hunt recalled a personal observation he made while speaking at a college in South America with regard to the effects of sin:

> It is (like) one of those great oceangoing cargo ships coming into the harbor that is met by a pilot-boat (tugboat); the pilot-boat in turn secures a towrope to the larger ship. At this time the helmsman releases all steering control to the pilot-boat and is now completely at the mercy of the one towing him.

This is how it is when we willingly allow something seemingly so small, like sin, to take over in our lives—it takes us into tow and we are now at the mercy of where it leads. If we stay focused on the things of God, there will be no room for sinful things to emerge. An olive tree is only protected from blight and parasites when it stays firmly rooted in the Farmer's grove, so He is able to be near to cultivate, water, nourish, and watch over it.

• Resist the devil as Jesus did in the wilderness. Jesus was not a wimp; He did not go out into the wilderness to cower down in a defensive posture while the devil beat up on Him. No, Jesus went out in the power of the Holy Spirit slapping down the devil with the Word of God. James 4:7 says, "Resist the devil and he will flee from you." I want you to have the attitude of a cop. Think of yourself as a cop— when there is a battle and the regular citizens are fleeing, you charge in to meet the threat. This does not mean you should go looking for a fight; it means you should do what the shepherd boy David did: meet the enemy with the power of the Word of God. I played soccer as a kid, but I'm well acquainted with the old football adage: the best defense is a strong offense. Remember, the devil has been defeated! This means that when the desire mysteriously surfaces to go play on your shiny new boat during Sunday morning worship, or when you have the thought, "Why is it wrong to put myself first?" you can fire back at the devil just as Jesus did, "It is written, 'You shall worship the Lord your God and serve

Him only'" (Luke 4:8). The olive tree's roots grow wide and deep, so that when the storms of life come or the devil comes attacking, you will be able to stand firm.

- Know who you are in Christ: you are a son or daughter of the Most High God! Paul reminded the Galatians in 4:6–7, "And because you are sons, God has sent forth the Spirit of His Son into our hearts, crying, Abba! Father! Therefore you are no longer a slave but a son; and if a son, then an heir through God." God waited until last to create man to reflect His glory, you are the prize fruit of His creation. Do you get it? You were not created to whimper before a defeated enemy: the devil is like a roaring lion, but he is not a roaring lion. The devil has no power over you, as you are a son or daughter of the Most High God! Therefore, pull yourself up by the bootstraps and proclaim who you are in Christ, and the devil will go looking for someone else to harass. You are an olive tree in God's royal olive grove, where only the choicest, handpicked trees are grown.

- After you committed yourself to begin working on your personal discipline, you must go to your pastor or whoever assigns people to different ministries, and present yourself to serve. The gospel of John records in 13:5–15 that at the Lord's supper, Jesus took water and washed the disciples' feet. Verses 14 and 15 recorded Jesus's words, "If I then, the Lord and the Teacher, washed your feet, you also ought to wash one another's feet. For I gave you an example that you also should do as I did to you." Jesus also states in Matthew 20:28, "Just as the Son of Man did not come to be served, but to serve, and to give His life a ransom for many." Jesus always modeled how believers should live their lives by living it Himself before them. If God really lives inside of our hearts then we will want to love and serve others just as Jesus did. The olive principle is about fruit (gifting with purpose) going forward to serve others, not clinging to the branch and dying. Ask the Holy Spirit (the Oil Master) to reveal what you are good at or enjoy doing and a ministry that can use your particular gifting. Then if you do not know how to do something, bug someone until they teach you. Then submit to the olive press.

Pastor Lay asked our congregation one Sunday, "Can you imagine what would happen if every Christian would spend time alone with God each day: there would not be room for those coming to Christ within our church." That is the end result of following the steps I have laid out for you. You would be out there following Jesus's teaching; you are the salt of the world (your life is to make others thirst for what you have), and you are a light (the outward manifestation of God's presence inside you will draw people to Him).

This is the essence of the olive principle—God created you for a purpose within His Kingdom so that you could find what many spend their lives searching for: fulfillment and significance. God loved you so much that He sacrificed His Son for you on the cross. God brought you out of slavery, nourished and pruned you, gave you something worth living for. Finally, God brought you through all the temporary circumstances to maturity, so when trouble or the enemy tried to attack, you would be able to overcome the storms of life. God also had another purpose: He knew the only true path to significance is through your willingly laying down your desires (olive press) and serving others to glorify Him. I have never felt so fulfilled in my life than when I risked my life as a police officer to save a citizen, and then again when I learned this principle in laying down my desires for God's. When God's desires (loving and serving others) become your desires, you will reflect His glory to the world. When serving God's desires you will find not only fulfillment in Him but also the significance you crave. Remember 2 Corinthians 3:18: "But we all, with unveiled face beholding as in a mirror the glory of the Lord, are being transformed from glory to glory, just as from the Lord, the Spirit." Therefore, if you are ready, let us close out this adventure by learning what a true servant is.

Chapter Eight:
Now a Servant

Congratulations! I am proud of you, because if you are reading this final chapter then you have accepted the challenge of becoming a true servant of God. You have now come face-to-face with whatever was hindering you from being in the presence of God and whatever handcuffed you from reaching fulfillment in both your physical and spiritual life. You have made a commitment to:

- Spend time in the Word of God five days a week.

- Spend time in prayer and worship to your Creator and Master.

- Journal about what you have studied and about your conversations with God.

- Make yourself accountable to a mature and trustworthy Christian.

- Submit yourself to God's pruning of things in your life in order to produce much fruit.

- Keep your mind focused on the things of God throughout your day.

- Resist (oppose) the enemy.

- Accept who you are in Christ as part of the royal family.

- Finally, present yourself as a servant to the Master in the Kingdom of God.

If you have committed to doing this and you have a journal, I want you to write down each thing you are going to do and then sign your name at the bottom. This, my friend, is a personal pledge, and I have found in my experience most Christians would rather take a beating than break their word.

Now, let's get down to business as it is time to make the step of contacting your pastor or whoever assigns people to the different ministries and proclaim as Isaiah did, "Here am I." Take some time to think about your personal gifts: What are you really good at? What just gets you excited? Or where is the greatest need? When I first stepped up to serve, I took care of watering the outside flowers and trimming the shrubs (displaying small buds). I then moved up to helping mop floors and began serving as a children's pastor while I was in ministry school. In my heart it was all about serving Jesus and making Him proud of me (growing fruit). You see, it did not matter what the job was, as I learned in 1 Corinthians 12:4–27 that every part of the Body of Christ is equally important: whether the eye, or the feet, or even those members of the body that are considered less honorable.

What is a servant anyway? I look around the secular world and see the example of people in law enforcement, firefighters, and those brave men and women in our armed forces. These are people who at any moment would lay down their hopes, dreams, and even their actual lives for another human being. "Greater love has no one than this that one lay down his life for his friends" (John 15:13). These are regular, imperfect people who hear a call in their heart, not to ministry, but to be a devoted servant to their communities and country. Is this about having super-human bravery? No, it is about people who see themselves as servants and have adopted these attitudes as their lifestyles.

> ## Jesus displayed the "attitude" of being a servant.

A servant is defined as a person bound to do the bidding of a master or superior, one that must work for another and obey him, one that performs duties about the person or home of a master or employer, or a personal or domestic attendant. The Bible gives a similar, yet more spiritual explanation (and expectation) of a servant in James 1:1, "James, a bond servant of God and of the Lord Jesus Christ." The term "bond servant" is translated from the Greek word *doulov*, which describes "the status of a slave or an 'attitude' corresponding to that of a slave." The bond servant has developed an attitude of willingly enslaving or chaining himself to the Lord. The bond servant sees himself without personal rights before God—His will is his desire. The bond servant is committed to the lifelong work of the Lord (submitting to being cultivated, watered, nourished, pruned, and to bearing fruit) without the need for personal glory. The New Testament's use of the word "servant" is seen in John 13:1–17, in the description of the Last Supper, and of Jesus's washing the feet of his disciples. The Greek usage here of the word servant makes it crystal clear that Jesus displayed the "attitude" of being a servant rather than striving for personal power or glory. Remember the model of Jesus in the Garden of Gethsemane? This is what being a true servant of God is all about—your "attitude" or how you see yourself in relation to Him. If you are willing to lay down your desires (olive press) at His feet, then you have the attitude of a servant and will be selected as choice oil.

James understood this attitude in that he owned nothing and had no authority, but everything he had, everything he was, and everything he accomplished—in essence his personal identity— was a reflection of his Master. This attitude was voluntary. James allowed the crushing of his self to Jesus and His will. Was this attitude always present with James? Hardly! If you study John 7:3–5, you would see that Jesus's brothers, including James, did not believe in Him as the Christ. James had to go through the same process of the olive principle that you and I must journey through: surrendering our lives to Jesus (become an olive tree) and allowing Him to water, nourish, cultivate, and prune our lives. We must allow our roots to grow wide and deep through the inward working of the Holy Spirit, in order to accomplish the Farmer's joy of reaping a harvest of much fruit in our lives.

I'm willing to take the risk of being redundant, because I want you to get this inside of you: being a true servant of God is about your "attitude" or how you see yourself in relation to Him. If you are willing to lay down your desire for personal glory at His feet, then you have the attitude of a servant. Again, *it is a process,* just as explained in the process of the olive principle, with the final desire of God that you would reach maturity. With maturity comes the desire to allow the "self," or the I factor, to be crushed, to deal with the impurities within your life, and to submit to the purpose of the gifting inside of you—to benefit people for the Kingdom. There is no fast track or way around the process; there is only steady growth in the things of God and the joyful discovery that you are a willing bond servant of God. It is in God's olive grove that you will find personal fulfillment (in) Him, and the significance that all of us need. David wrote in Psalm 52:8–9, "I am like a green olive tree in the house of God; I trust in the mercy of God forever and ever. I will praise you forever, Because You have done it; And in the presence of Your saints I will wait on Your name, for it is good" (NKJV). Is this not what this whole book was about, surrendering your self-will to the Father and putting others first so that you might be a reflection of Him? Paul wrote in 2 Corinthians 3:3, "You are a letter from Christ, the result of our ministry, written not with ink but with the Spirit of the living God, not on tablets of stone but on tablets of human hearts" (NIV).

> # A bond servant is what I
> # want my identity to be.

A bond servant is what I want my personal identity to be, so in faith I close all my letters by signing, "A bond servant of God." Have I arrived at the level of the Apostle Paul or James? Am I where I want to be? No, but I am submitting myself to the Farmer's (God's) process of cultivating, watering, nourishing, and pruning, so my roots will grow wide and deep. Then the fruit I bear of serving the unchurched and the Body of Christ will display that of a bond servant. Is not loving one another the heart of the servant of God? Plant your roots deep within God, stay focused on the work of the Farmer, and you will touch someone's life.

In closing, I am reminded of a mass e-mail I received years ago that told the story of a woman who was searching for fulfillment. The woman came upon an old silversmith and asked if she could watch him at his trade, to which he agreed. The old silversmith took a lump of silver ore from a bag and placed it in an iron tool. In turn, the tool and ore were inserted into a furnace of fire. The woman in her curiosity asked what was planned for this lump of ore, and the old silversmith replied that he planned to make different items: some for grand use and some for common use. The woman watched as the ore melted—once the molten ore was liquefied it was pulled out of the fire briefly so the impurities (dross) could be removed, then into the fire again it went. The silversmith repeated this action a second and then a third time, and when curiosity once again overtook the woman she asked, "When do you know the silver is ready for use?" "Oh, that is easy," said the wise old silversmith, "I know it is ready when I can see my reflection." This is what Jesus was on the earth—the reflection of the Father. Are you ready to let your face shine again and be His reflection to a dying world?

Bibliography

Arthur, Kay. *How To Study Your Bible.* Eugene, OR: Harvest House Publishers, 1994.

Bonhoeffer, Dietrich. *The Cost of Discipleship.* New York: Touchstone Books, 1995.

Coleman, Robert E. *The Master Plan of Evangelism.* Grand Rapids, MI: Revell Books, 2010.

Hunt, Larry D. *An Exposition of the Book of James.* Baton Rouge, LA: World Evangelism Press, 1993.

Kempis, Thomas à. *The Imitation of Christ.* San Francisco: Ignatius Press, 2005.